Demystifying the World of Ethical Hacking

Stephen N. Arnold

Contents

3

4

Following the completion of the repair, a validation scan is carried out to check and ensure that the security flaws have been effectively fixed.

6

10

Introduction to Ethical Hacking

Unveiling the Digital Guardian and Providing an Introduction to Ethical Hacking, the digital domain has evolved into both a boon and a conflict in our modern day, when technology affects every facet of our lives. The significance of protecting our digital assets has never been more prevalent than it is now, as the global community continues to grow more influential. Ethical hacking, a discipline characterized by its mysticism and allure, might be seen as having its origins in this setting.

1. Origins of Ethical Hacking

The word "hacker" sometimes evokes mental pictures of serious people skulking in the shadows to penetrate security systems for malicious reasons. Ethical hacking is a striking contrast to this picture; it is a method that uses the talents and strategies of hackers for excellent and productive reasons. While this image is accurate for some, it is not precise for others.

2. Definition of Ethical Hacking

Ethical hacking, known as penetration testing or white-hat hacking, is a proactive approach to resolving cyber security vulnerabilities. Other names for this kind of hacking are ethical hacking and white-hat hacking. In this hypothetical situation, authorized individuals inside a company—typically those working in cyber security—consciously try to breach the organization's security systems. What precisely is it that they want to accomplish? To prevent malicious hackers from taking advantage of flaws, gaps, and potential threats, to discover such loopholes, cracks, and possible dangers.

3. Toolkit for Ethical Hackers

Ethical hackers draw from a comprehensive toolset of abilities and strategies to successfully negate the complex dynamic between security and vulnerability. They explore the role of computer systems, networks, and applications to locate vulnerabilities that may result in data breaches or assaults.

4. Understanding hacker mentality

When ethical hackers enter the digital space, they develop a maturity similar to unethical hackers. They have to put themselves in their opponents' shoes and try to anticipate possible attack vectors, then exploit those vectors before they can be used to damage. On the other hand, this way of thinking is moderated by a firm dedication to ethical ideals and a strong sense of duty.

5. Legal and moral environment

The practice of ethical hacking is not an organized activity. It does it within the confines of a legally and morally sound framework that has been meticulously designed. Because breaking into computer systems without proper authority is a criminal offence, obtaining permission is paramount. Companies often use contractual agreements to bring on ethical hackers and provide such individuals with specific references to assess the effectiveness of the organization's security procedures.

6. The Goals of Ethical Hacking

Enhancing a network's or computer system's level of security is the primary focus of ethical hacking. Organizations may take proactive steps to boost their defences if they first identify the vulnerabilities and flaws that exist in their systems. Ethical hackers are also involved in the incident response process, which aims to assist businesses in recovering from security breaches with as little disruption as possible.

7. Scope and Domains of Ethical Hacking

Ethical hacking is a broad field that encompasses various areas due to its expanse and complexity. Network security, internal application security, cloud security, mobile device security, and other types of protection are included in this category. Ethical hackers may specialize in one or more of these areas, improving their abilities to handle certain dangers.

8. The Role of Certification

The field of ethical hacking places a premium on knowledge and experience. Several certification programs offer training and validation of abilities, including Certified Ethical Hacker (CEH) and Certified Information Systems Security Professional (CISSP). Within the field of cyber security, these certificates have a very high level of protection.

9. The Cat and Mouse Game

Hackers with good intentions and hackers with bad intentions are always playing a cat-and-mouse game in the constantly shifting world of cyber security. Ethical hackers always uncover new vulnerabilities, while bad actors continually adapt and look for new exploits. This dynamic interaction highlights the continual need for awareness and creativity in cyber security. Cyber security is an ever-evolving discipline.

10. The Ethical Hacker's Code

Ethical hackers must abide by a stringent code of conduct that emphasizes integrity and security while mandating a commitment to responsible disclosure. They provide rapid and detailed reports of their findings to the businesses they invest in, establishing severe corruption.

11. The Future of Ethical Hacking

Ethical hacking will only become more important as time passes because of how quickly technology is progressing. The number of potential enterprise points for malicious actors is growing due to the growth of Internet of Things (Iota) devices, cloud computing, and networked systems. Protecting our digital future will be significantly aided by the work of ethical hackers.

The Hacker Mindset

There is a one-thousand-word article on "The Hacker Mindset" that does not violate any copyright restrictions: Uncovering the Mysterious World of Ethical Hacking through the Lens of the Hacker Mindset In the world of information technology and computer security, there is a unique and mysterious subculture of people known as hackers. These people have a distinct personality that breeds curiosity, initiative, and a profound comprehension of technological concepts. Hackers have often been characterized as malicious people aiming to exploit flaws, but reality is more complicated than this portrayal suggests. Ethical hackers, in particular, support a methodology that provides sensitive information and secures digital environments for the greater good. To understand the nature of a hacker, one must first debunk the myths and misconceptions surrounding this subculture. Hackers are often depicted in popular culture as shadowy characters wearing hoods and bent over computer screens in poorly lit rooms while rapidly typing in an attempt to bypass security measures. Despite their ability to make movies, these responses fall short of capturing the true nature of ethical hacking.

The hacker mentality is characterized by a need for knowledge at its very foundation. Ethical hackers are motivated by an unquestionable desire to learn how computer systems operate, solve the mysteries surrounding technology, and find security flaws in software and hardware before dishonest parties can exploit them. Their natural curiosity motivates them to learn new things and their commitment to working in the cyber security industry. Hackers are people who want information, and as a result, they often have an innovative approach to problem-solving. They don't see difficulties as insurmountable barriers; instead, they see them as puzzles that must be solved. Because of their creativity, they can think in novel ways, recognize security flaws that others may miss, and develop original solutions to complex security problems. The attitude of a hacker also has a strong sense of personal responsibility. Hackers who practice ethics are aware of the potential danger that bad actors may pose to companies and society. They believe it is their ethical responsibility to contribute to improving cyber security, the defence of digital infrastructure, and the protection of sensitive data. The ability to welcome ambiguity and adjust one's behaviour in response to changing circumstances is essential to hacker maturity. Hackers are aware that the cyber security environment is constantly shifting, which means that what is safe today may not be secure tomorrow. They never stop acquiring new knowledge and keep themselves current with the latest technology, vulnerabilities, and attack methodologies. To effectively combat cyber-attacks, flexibility of this kind is essential. Transparency and cooperation are also highly valued by ethical hackers. They are firm believers in the need for exchanging information, working in conjunction with others, and cooperating to boost the network's security. This strong sense of community is one of the defining characteristics of the hacker community, and it is a factor that helps to expand the profession.

Additionally, ethical hackers have a rigorous moral code that they abide by. They abhor values such as honesty, respect for others' privacy, and integrity in everything they do. When performing security inspections, they are dedicated to doing so in compliance with the law and after obtaining the appropriate authority. Their differences protect them from dishonest hackers by having an ethical basis. The hacker mentality encompasses more than just technological evolution. It involves having a profound sense of responsibility and dedication to making the digital world more secure for everyone. Typical jobs ethical hackers hold include penetration testers, security analysts, and cyber security consultants. They can detect vulnerabilities, evaluate risks, and recommend repair techniques using their methods. The capacity to see technology as a tool for making the world a better place is one of the most essential characteristics of a hacker's attitude. Ethical hackers recognize the opportunities for innovation and advancement presented by technology. They are committed to ensuring that it is utilized responsively while maintaining its level of safety. They have faith in the ability of technology to disrupt whole sectors, improve people's lives, and propel social progress forward.

Legal and Ethical Considerations

1. The Legal Landscape

Ethical hacking, often known as "white hat hacking," is when authorized people or teams try to uncover vulnerabilities in computer systems, networks, and applications. Ethical hacking is also sometimes referred to as "black hat hacking." Even if the goal of ethical hackers is to improve security, their acts often overlap with activities that might be considered unlawful if they are not carried out within the parameters of the law. While the objectives of ethical hackers are admirable, they do not always follow the law. Acquiring the necessary permission is one of the most essential parts of ethical hacking. Even when done with the best of intentions, unauthorized access to computer systems may have serious legal consequences. Before doing any testing or vulnerability assessment, ethical hackers must obtain permission from the owner or administrator of the system. If this is not done, criminal charges may arise, including hacking, unlawful access, and data breaches. In addition, ethical hackers are responsible for complying with the rules and regulations that regulate the protection of personal information and privacy. Handling and protecting sensitive data is subject to strict rules imposed by laws such as the General Data Protection Regulation (GDPR) in the European Union and the Health Insurance Portability and Accountability Act (HIPAA) in the United States. Both of these pieces of legislation were enacted in 2018. Ethical hackers are required to have knowledge of these rules and to ensure that their activities comply with them.

2. Ethical Considerations

Beyond legal requirements, ethical hackers follow a set of moral principles. These principles emphasize integrity, security, and ethical hacking.

- **Integrity:**

Hackers with ethical intentions are expected to operate with unquestionable integrity continuously. They should never take part in actions that put the confidence that the system's owners have placed them in jeopardy. They need to carry out their task diligently and transparently.

- **Confidentiality:**

During ethical hacking examinations, one often obtains information that is considered very sensitive. Ethical hackers are responsible for maintaining the strictest levels of security regarding this information. Unauthorized replication of data breaches or vulnerabilities may have significant ramifications for the organization.

- **Responsible Disclosure:**

Ethical hackers who identify vulnerabilities must swiftly communicate their discoveries to the owner of the system in which they discovered the vulnerability. This process of responsible disclosure guarantees that vulnerabilities are recognized and not exploited by hostilities in any way.

- **Minimize Harm:**

Hackers who play by the rules should always try to do the most minor damage possible to their target systems and networks. Their objective is to locate security flaws without causing any interruption or physical harm. If there are circumstances in which interruption cannot be avoided, then it must be carried out with the most excellent care and prudence.

- **Continuous Learning:**

The domain of cyber security is constantly evolving with new developments. Ethical hackers must participate in ongoing learning and professional development activities to stay current on the latest security flaws and dangers.

3. Challenges and Dilemmas

In the course of their jobs, ethical hackers often face challenging moral conundrums. The tension that exists between organization and steady tasting is a problem that many organizations face. Should a hacker who practices ethical hacking warn the system's owner, or is it more ethical to run a test that simulates a real-world attack without the owner's knowledge? The particulars of the situation, as well as the goals of the evaluation, should be taken into consideration while attempting to find a happy medium between the two methods. When ethical hackers identify vulnerabilities that might affect the firm or its consumers, this is another hurdle that must be overcome. They were tasked with navigating the tricky situation of reporting these vulnerabilities to the company and providing advice. To do this, one needs strong communication skills and a dedication to finding solutions to problems through cooperative effort.

Foot printing and Data Collection

"Foot printing and Data Collection" is one of the first steps in the ethical hacking process and one of the most critical steps. This phase lays the groundwork for subsequent phases, during which a target will be identified, vulnerabilities will be identified, and finally, the system will be secured. It is a procedure that calls for careful attention to every little detail and strict adhesions to ethical principles to guarantee that the lines between legal and moral are maintained.

1. Understanding foot printing:

The reconnaissance stage of military operations is sometimes analogized to foot writing because of its similarities. Collecting information on a target, whether that target is an individual, an organization, or a network, is an essential part of this process. The objective here is not to make malicious use of this information but to evaluate the security posture and locate any possible vulnerability.

2. Types of Information Gathered:

Ethical hackers collect a wide variety of information during the foot printing phase, which may be arranged into a few primary categories depending on the nature of the data.

• Publicly Available Information:

This comprises information available to the general public and may be found on corporate websites, social media accounts, and public records, among other places. It may provide information about the organization's hierarchy, most important employees, and technological infrastructure.

- **Network Information:**
Hackers with good intentions try to learn the structure of the network as well as its IP addresses, domain names, and subdomains. The latter steps of the penetration tasting will need this knowledge.

- **System Details:**
It is necessary to have information on the target systems' operating systems, software vulnerabilities, and symptoms to identify possible vulnerabilities successfully.

- **Employee Information:**
During socially engaging assaults, in which the attackers try to persuade people into divulging sensitive information, it may be helpful to get insights into workers' roles, their email addresses and other contact information.

- **Security Measures:**
By understanding the security mechanisms currently in place, such as firewalls, intrusion detection systems, and encryption techniques, one may have a better understanding of the amount of protection the target has.

3. Methods of Data Collection:

Ethical hackers depend on a variety of approaches to get this information, including both passive and active strategies, such as the following:

- **Passive foot printing**

This entails gathering intelligence without directly contacting the investigation's subject. Examples include looking for information on public sectors, social media platforms, and social engineering.

- **Active foot printing**

In this scenario, the ethical hacker collects information on the target by directly interacting with the target's computer systems. These techniques include DNS sequences, trace routes, and network scanning.

Scanning and Enumeration

Unveiling the Mysticism of Network Discovery Through the use of scanning and enumeration Scanning and enumeration have emerged as crucial methods in the world of ethical hacking, which is the practice of protecting digital landscapes from malicious invaders via the use of hacking techniques that are not malevolent. Although these procedures may seem technical and arcane, they play a critical role in recognizing the weaknesses that hackers may attack and in strengthening those flaws. In this discussion, we dig into the fascinating realm of scanning and enumeration, illuminating their relevance and methodology while highlighting the importance of their use in ethical and legal contexts.

1. The Meaning of Scanning and Enumeration

The reconnaissance stage of ethical hacking consists of many stages, the most basic of which are scanning and execution. When assessing the security posture of a network or system, these are the first steps that are taken. While they are working toward the same end goal, which is the identification of any loopholes, the approaches they use and the information they try to get from the system are quite different.

2. Scanning: Unveiling the Network Topology

The initial part of this process, scanning, is analogous to a digital cartographer exploring unexplored territory. The primary purpose of this tool is to determine the network's topology by locating active hosts, operating ports, and services operating on those servers. Ethical hackers have given a map of the web due to this knowledge, which is analogous to finding out the architecture of a castle before constructing a design for it. The port scanner is an essential piece of equipment that is used throughout the scanning process. Sending packets to a target system's many ports to discover which ports are open and responsive is an essential step in the port scanning process. TCP connection scans, SYN scans, and UDP scans are examples of port scanning techniques. These scans give vital insights into the services operating on offshore ports, enabling security specialists to identify possible risks associated with the scanned services.

3. Enumeration: Extracting Valuable Data

When the network's topology has been discovered by scanning, the next step is enumeration. Enumeration is a process that seeks to extract particular information from various services and systems; it is not limited to just locating open ports. This method is analogous to looking through the windows of the stronghold to obtain information about the actions of the people who live there. Interacting with the services and systems is required for enumeration to get information such as user accounts, shares, network resources, and configuration information. Techniques such as SNMP, DNS, and SMB enumeration are standard. By using these tactics, ethical hackers can get a more in-depth comprehension of the network's structure and the possible weak areas it may include.

4. The Moral and Legal System

Although scanning and enumeration are crucial weapons in the armoury of an ethical hacker, their use must be governed by robust ethical and legal frameworks to avoid ethical and legal repercussions. The purpose of ethical hacking is not to inflict damage or disruption but rather to uncover weaknesses and provide solutions to fix them. Therefore, acquiring the appropriate permission is of the utmost importance. If they want to scan and encode a system or network, ethical hackers should always get permission from the owners or administrators of that system or network before proceeding. Unauthorized scanning and enumeration can result in legal repercussions since these activities might be considered intruding and hateful acts. Additionally, those who hack responsively should despise the notion of responsive disclosure. When vulnerabilities are found, they should be communicated to the appropriate parties responsively and appropriately. This will allow the proper parties to take steps to address the problem.

5. Scanning and Enumeration in Practice

Consider the following example, which will help explain the practical use of scanning and enumeration: a business wishes to evaluate the level of security practised by its internal network. Following receipt of the necessary permission, the ethical hacker starts the process by doing a network scan using several different scanning methods. The scan indicates the existence of several hosts, some of which are running out-of-date services that are susceptible to known vulnerabilities. The ethical hacker then moves on to the next step of the process: enumerate the benefits, extract information from user accounts, and locate possible weak spots. As a result of having access to this information, the business is now in a position to take proactive steps to patch or upgrade vulnerable services, change weak passwords, and improve the overall security of its network.

Vulnerability Assessment

Vulnerability Assessment: Building a Stronger Defense for Cyberspace The need to practice good cyber security cannot be overemphasized in a world that is becoming more and more linked, where digital landscapes are increasingly serving as the basis for information and resources. To protect themselves against the ever-shifting nature of the third environment, people, organizations, and even governments need to strengthen their defences. Vulnerability Assessment is a proactive method that plays a critical role in detecting and adding possible flaws in information systems. It is one of the most crucial aspects of this defence, and it is one of the most essential aspects of this defence. In this article, we will introduce the meaning of the term "vulnerability assessment," its relevance, the methodology used to conduct vulnerability assessments, and its role in improving cyber security.

1. Understanding Vulnerabilities

Before getting into vulnerability, it is necessary to have a solid understanding of what exactly vulnerabilities are. A weakness or fault in a system, application, or network that hostile actors might exploit is referred to as a vulnerability in the field of cyber security. Vulnerabilities can be used in a variety of ways. All of these vulnerabilities may leave an organization's digital assets vulnerable to attack, and they can take the form of software defects, corrupt systems, or even weaknesses in the system's architecture.

2. The Value of Vulnerability Assessment

In cyber security, the vulnerability assessment is the first line of defence. Its primary objective is to locate computer system security flaws before malicious hackers exploit them. When this is done, it enables businesses to take proactive steps, strengthening their overall security posture. The age-old proverb "You can't fix what you don't know is broken" rings especially true in cyber security. The Vulnerability Assessment brings to light previously concealed weaknesses, allowing for the possibility of repairing such flaws before potentially harmful parties may exploit them.

3. Vulnerability Assessment Methods

When assessing a system's, networks, or application's level of vulnerability, various research approaches and diagnostic tools are used. The following are the two primary strategies that may be used while using these methodologies:

- **Network-Based Vulnerability Assessment:**

This strategy focuses on scanning and analyzing network components, including routers, switches, and servers, to find vulnerabilities in a network. Network scanners, which are often automated, are used to find open ports, outdated software vulnerabilities, and possible misconfigurations that attackers might exploit. These vulnerabilities could be exploited in many different ways.

- **Host-Based Vulnerability Assessment:**

In contrast to network-based evaluation, this technique focuses on individual host systems, such as servers, workstations, and mobile devices. It entails scanning the host's operating system and the software put on it to identify vulnerabilities such as unpatched applications, weak passwords, and insecure sessions.

4. The Vulnerability Assessment Process

In most cases, the process of vulnerability assessment will consist of the following significant steps:

- **Asset Identification:**

First, it is necessary to document all of the assets included in the organization's network. This pertains to the hardware, software, and data stores.

- **Vulnerability Scanning:**

Automated technologies are used to perform a vulnerability scan on previously identified assets. These programs examine the status of the system and the various software versions compared to a database of known vulnerabilities.

- **Vulnerability Analysis:**

When a vulnerability has been discovered, it is followed by an analysis to determine its possible consequences and the chance it will be exploited. Because not all vulnerabilities provide the same amount of danger, choosing which ones to

Prioritize is essential.

- **Remediation:**

The evaluation results are used by businesses to formulate a strategy for mitigating unknown risks. Implementing software fixes, re-configuring systems, or tightening access restrictions might all be necessary.

Validation:

Following the completion of the repair, a validation scan is carried out to check and ensure that the security flaws have been effectively fixed.

5. Assessment of Vulnerabilities Faces Difficulties

Even though vulnerability Assessment is an essential component of cyber security, it presents its unique set of difficulties. There can be false positives and negatives, which is when the assessment tools either wrongly identify vulnerabilities that do not exist (known as false positives) or overlook valid vulnerabilities (known as false negatives). In addition, since new vulnerabilities were found and exploited by cybercriminals at such a rapid rate, it is imperative that attackers be carried out regularly to ensure continued safety.

Exploitation Techniques

In the context of ethical hacking, the phrase "exploitation techniques" may have a sinister ring to it, evoking thoughts of malicious hackers breaking into computer networks and wreaking havoc on the data contained in them. On the other hand, in the white-hat hacking domain, exploitation methods are an essential part of locating vulnerabilities, building up security, and effectively protecting digital assets from being subjected to harmful assaults. This article goes into the world of execution tactics, illuminating their reliability, the methodology they use, and the ethical concerns that arise from using them. The simulation of actual online assaults is at the heart of ethical hacking, which seeks to pinpoint any computer network or system vulnerability. Exploitation methods are the tools and strategies ethical hackers use to illustrate their uncovered vulnerabilities. These techniques are also known as "hacking techniques." These methods are only a means to an end; the ultimate objective is to patch, secure, and defend the systems that are being installed. There is a widespread misunderstanding that ethical hackers intentionally inflict damage using these methods.

On the other hand, they have good intentions to resolve security flaws in software before criminals can take advantage of them. This proactive strategy is essential to cyber security because it helps avoid data breaches and prevents sensitive information from being compromised. "exploitation techniques" refer to various methods and tools, each designed to exploit a particular kind of vulnerability or attack vector. This section will introduce some of the core strategies that ethical hackers use.

- **Buffer Overflow Attacks:**

Attacks targeting software vulnerabilities using the buffer overflow technique are among the oldest and most well-known execution methods. Hackers can alter a program's functionality, and sometimes, they get unauthorized access if they cause it to overflow with an excessive amount of data.

- **SQL Injection:**

Databases are the targets of assaults using SQL injection. Hackers may manipulate databases to divulge sensitive information or obtain unauthorized access by inserting malicious SQL queries into input fields.

- **Cross-Site Scripting (XSS):**

Attacks using cross-site scripting (XSS) exploit security flaws in online applications. Attackers can steal data from users or take actions on their behalf without their knowledge or consent if they inject malicious scripts into web sites.

- **Phishing:**

Phishing is a method of deceiving people into giving sensitive information, such as passwords or credit card numbers. Phishing is not a technical exploit technique; it depends on social engineering to accomplish this goal. Ethical hackers often evaluate a business to see its vulnerability to phishing attacks.

- **Privilege Escalation:**

Acquiring more permissions or privileges without a computer system or network is the goal of this method. Hackers with a moral code make it their mission to intercept their access permissions to expose possible security flaws that might allow unauthorized users to take control of a system.

• Remote Code Execution

Hackers who don't break the law look for security holes in computer systems that might let them run programs remotely on their target systems. This might lead to complete control over the system that was infiltrated.

• Zero-Day Exploits:

There are flaws in the software or hardware that the manufacturer is unaware of, and as a result, no patches are available for them. Ethical hackers may sometimes find zero-day vulnerabilities and appropriately report them to manufacturers to assist businesses in securing their products.

• Password Cracking:

Hackers with a moral compass put the security of a system critical to the test by using password-cracking methods. Because of this, corporations can effectively enforce more onerous password restrictions.

- **Man-in-the-Middle (MITM) Attacks:**

Intercepting and potentially altering the communication between two parties is the goal of MITM attacks. Ethical hackers use these methods to illustrate the flaws in the security of a network.

- **Denial of Service (Do) Attacks:**

Testing a system's resistance to denial-of-service attacks might be considered an example of ethical hacking, even though such testing is not usually conducted ethically. The capability of a plan to withstand heavy loads and continue functioning generally without an assault is evaluated using this method. When using various forms of extortion, ethical hackers must follow strict regulations and stay within the bounds of the law. They often conduct their business with the express permission of the system's owner and within the confines of relevant laws and regulations. This guarantees that not only are their behaviours moral, but they are also within the law. In addition, one of the most essential ethical hacking techniques is the concept of responsible disclosure. Ethical hackers work collaboratively with corporations to quickly disclose and repair any vulnerabilities discovered after conducting vulnerability assessments. This coordination is vital to ensure that vulnerabilities are addressed before criminal actors can take advantage of them.

Password Cracking and Authentication

It is of the utmost significance to provide access to this data in this era of digitization, where private and sensitive information is regularly stored and exchanged via digital networks. In the realm of the internet, passwords are an essential part of the authentication process. They are the equivalent of the keys to our digital homes. Nevertheless, the efficacy of security that is dependent on a password is contingent not only on the toughness of passwords but also on the mechanisms that are used for authentication. This article digs deep into password cracking and authentication complications, illuminating the critical parts of protecting our digital assets and providing a better understanding of how they work.

1. Authentication and Its Significance

A user's, a system's, or an entity's identity may be verified by a process known as authentication, which pertains to computer security. The government is responsible for ensuring that only authorized people or computer systems can access the protected resources. Using a username and password to authenticate is the method that is used most often. Users validate their identities by supplying a unique identifier (a user name) and a secure code (a password). It is impossible to stress how important it is to have authentication. Unauthorized accounts, data breaches, and the exposure of sensitive information are all potential outcomes of authentication measures that are inadequate or that have been hacked. For this reason, the robustness of authentication mechanisms and the security of passwords are essential in protecting the confidentiality and integrity of digital assets.

2. The Role of Passwords

Numerous online services and systems rely heavily on using passwords as the primary authentication method. As a result of the ease with which people can understand them and the relative ease with which they can be implemented, they are a popular option for user authentication. However, the efficacy of passwords depends on the difficulty of the passwords themselves and the security measures in place to secure them. Weak passwords pose a threat to the system's security. A short phrase, a string of randomly generated letters (like "123456"), or information that is easy to deduce, such as a birthday, are all examples of poor password choices. Hackers often use various methods to crack passwords; this is where the term "password cracking" comes into play.

3. Password Cracking

The act of trying to decrypt or recover a password from its encrypted form is referred to as "password cracking." Hackers use a wide variety of strategies and tools to break passwords. These strategies may vary from simple brute-force assaults to more complex ways.

- **Brute Force Attack:**

In a brute force attack, the attacker will try every possible combination of characters until they find the correct password. This approach requires a lot of time and resources, but it helps crack passwords that aren't very strong.

- **Dictionary Attack:**

An attack known as a dictionary attack includes tasting a collection of words and phrases that are often used as possible passwords. It is a method that is more efficient than brute force and can be successful if the password is based on a popular term.

- **Rainbow Tables:**

Rainbow tables are tables of password hashes that have been precomputed. These tabs allow attackers to rapidly split up the hash of a password and locate the corresponding plaintext password.

- **Phishing:**

Phishing attacks include misleading consumers into divulging their credentials by impeaching a trusted organization. This is often accomplished via the use of fraudulent emails or websites.

4. Strengthening Password Security

It is essential to develop robust password rules and use best practices to reduce the risks associated with password cracking.

- **Complexity Requirements:**

It should be mandatory to use passwords that satisfy compatibility requirements, such as having a combination of capital and lowercase letters, digits, and special characters.

- **Password Length:**

In general, having a longer password is better for your security. Users should be encouraged to generate longer passwords rather than short passwords that are easy to guess.

- **Two-Factor Authentication (2FA):**
By requiring users to submit a second form of authentication, such as an on-time code delivered to their mobile device, implementing two-factor authentication (also known as 2FA) provides an extra layer of protection to the system.

- **Regular Password Changes**
Users should be encouraged to change their passwords regularly to reduce the possibility of unwanted accounts.

Web Application Security

In today's interconnected world, web applications have become integral to our daily lives. From online banking and shopping to social media and email, we rely heavily on web applications for various tasks. However, this increasing dependency on web apps makes us vulnerable to cyber threats. Web application security is paramount to safeguarding our digital interactions and sensitive information.

1. Understanding Web Application Vulnerabilities

Web applications are complex systems with numerous components and functionalities. As a result, they often contain vulnerabilities that malicious actors can exploit. These vulnerabilities can be broadly classified into several types:

- **Injection Attacks**

Attackers inject malicious code or scripts into input files, such as SQL injection or cross-site scripting (XSS) attacks, to manipulate the application's behaviour.

- **Broken Authentication:**

Weak or broken authentication mechanisms can allow unauthorized access to user accounts and sensitive data.

- **Insecure Deserialization**

Attackers can manipulate serialized data to execute arbitrary code, potentially compromising the application.

- **Security Misconfigurations:**
Poorly configured security settings, passwords, or error handling can expose sensitive information or provide avenues for attacks.

- **Sensitive Data Exposure:**
Inadequate encryption or improper handling of sensitive data can lead to breaches and privacy violations.

- **Mitigating web application threats**
Protecting web applications from these vulnerabilities requires a multi-layered approach to security. There are some key strategies:

- **Input Validation:**
Implement strict input validation to prevent injection attacks. Validate and sanitize user inputs to ensure they do not contain malicious code.

- **Authentication and Authorization:**
Use robust authentication methods, such as multi-factor authentication (MFA), and enforce access controls to restrict user privileges.

- **Regular Patching:**
Keep all components and departments of the Web application up to date with security patches. Attackers can exploit vulnerabilities in third-party libraries.

- **Security Headers:**

Use security headers like Content Security Policy (CSP) and HTTP Strict Transport Security (HSTS) to control how browsers handle content and ensure secure connections.

- **Web Application Firewalls (was)**
Employ was to filter and monitor incoming traffic, blocking malicious requests and mitigating known attack patterns.

- **Encryption:**
Use secure encryption protocols (e.g., HTTPS) to protect data in transit. Encrypt sensitive data first and use robust encryption algorithms.

2. The Role of Develops

Integrating security into the development process is crucial for adequate Web application security. Devsecops, an approach that combines development, operations, and security, emphasizes continuous security testing and automation. By incorporating security practices early in the development lifecycle, organizations can identify and address vulnerabilities before they become significant risks.

3. The Ongoing Battle

Web application security is not an on-time effort but an ongoing battle against evolving threats. As technology advances, so do the tactics of cybercriminals. Regular monitoring, intelligence, and incident response plans are essential to a proactive security posture.

Network Security

In an increasingly interconnected world, the importance of network security cannot be overstated. As the digital landscape expands, so do the threats that seek to exploit it. Network security, often called the core of cyber security, is the art and science of protecting computer networks and the data they transmit from unauthorized access, use, disclosure, disruption, modification, or destruction. In this essay, we will delve into the intricate intricacies of network security measures, their significance, and the ever-evolving landscape of the threats they must combat. The Burstyn's of Network Threats Networks are the backbone of modern communication and information exchange. They establish everything from online banking and e-commerce to social media and critical infrastructure control. However, they also provide a target for malicious actors. As networks have become more complex and interconnected, network threats have grown. Today's cybercriminals are equipped with sophisticated tools and techniques, making securing networks a formidable challenge. One of the primary goals of network security is to protect data confidentiality, integrity, and availability. Confidentiality ensures that only authorized individuals can access sensitive information. Integrity ensures that data remains unaltered during transmission or storage. Availability guarantees that data and network services are accessible when needed. Layers of Defense: The Irregular Fortification Network security employs a multi-layer defence approach, much like the layers of an onion. Each layperson serves as an additional barrier to potential threats, creating an irregular fortification that is more challenging for attackers to breach.

- **Perimeter Security:**

This is the ultimate layer of defence and includes measures like firewalls and intrusion detection systems (IDS). Firewalls act as gatekeepers, filtering incoming and outgoing traffic to block unauthorized access. IDS monitors network traffic for suspicious activity.

- **Access Control**

Within the network, access control mechanisms restrict who can access specific resources. This level includes techniques like user authentication and authorization.

- **Encryption:**

Encryption is converging data into a code to prevent unauthorized access. It ensures the confidentiality of data in transit. Secure Sockets Layer (SSL) and Transport Layer Security (TLS) are commonly used encryption protocols.

- **Network Monitoring:**

Continuous monitoring of network traffic is crucial. Security Information and Event Management (SIEM) systems detect and respond to security incidents in real-time.

- **Patch Management:**
Regularly updating and patching software and hardware vulnerabilities is essential. Attackers often exploit unpatched systems.

- **Security Policies and Training**
Educating employees about security best practices and implementing security policies is critical. Human error remains a significant threat vector. Evolution of Threats and Effective Strategies The field of network security is in a constant state of development. Criminals adapt and develop new techniques, necessitating a corresponding change in defensive strategies.

- **Advanced Persistent Threats (apt):**
Pats are long-term, highly sophisticated attacks typically conducted by nation-states or organized cybercrime groups. They often involve targeted social engagement and multiple stages of infiltration.

- **Ransom ware:**
Ransom ware attacks encrypt a victim's data and demand a ransom for encryption. Organizations must prepare robust backup and recovery strategies to mitigate the impact of ransom ware.

- **Iota Security:**
The proliferation of Internet of Things (Iota) devices introduces new vulnerabilities. Securing these devices is paramount to protecting them from becoming entry points for attackers.

- **Zero Trust Security:**
Zero trust is a security model that assumes no one inside or outside the network can be trusted. It requires strict access controls, continuous monitoring, and least privilege access.

- **Machine Learning and AI:**
These technologies analyze network traffic and identify anomalies in real-time, enabling faster temperature detection.

Wireless Network Security

Wireless network connections can be found anywhere in today's hyper-connected society, where the internet is the digital equivalent of a stable support structure for our everyday lives. Wi-Fi's penetration into our homes, workplaces, public spaces, and even coffee shops has fundamentally altered how we conduct business, communicate with others, and gain access to information. This communication does come with a catch, and that catch is the requirement that we have strong security for our wireless networks to protect our digital assets and sensitive information.

1. The Wireless Landscape: An Overview

Radio waves are the medium by which wireless networks, often known as Wi-Fi networks, transport data from one device to another. They allow users to connect to the inside without being physically connected to a connection, in contrast to wired networks, which do not provide this freedom of mobility. Because of its superior connectivity, Wi-Fi has become the new standard for home and commercial users.

2. The Importance of Wireless Network Security

As the use of wireless networks has grown, so has the needs for wireless network security. The digital landscape is fraught with threats, from data breaches and eavesdropping to unauthorized access and malware attacks. Without adequate protection, wireless networks become vulnerable points of entry for cybercriminals.

3. Securing Wireless Networks: Safeguarding Digital Communication

The proliferation of wireless networks has fundamentally altered how we acquire information and communicate. Our digital world has been transformed due to the prevalence of Wi-Fi, which can be found everywhere, from homes and companies to public and private locations. However, in preparing for this conference, a wide variety of security concerns are presented, all of which must be addressed. Acquiring Knowledge of the Dangers Unauthorized access is one of the critical concerns regarding the safety of wireless networks. Networks with insufficient security are vulnerable to being exploited by hackers and other hostile actors, who could obtain unauthorized access to critical data or launch assaults. Implementing strict safety precautions is necessary to prevent this danger. The use of encryption serves as the first defensive line. The use of encryption is essential to ensuring the security of wireless networks. It provides that any data that is transmitted over the network is unintelligent to anyone who does not possess the appropriate encryption. Robust encryption techniques, such as WPA3, must be utilized to safeguard data while it is in transit. Individualized Passwords: Enhancing

Security of Access Control A typical mistake that makes weak networks susceptible to attack is using defective passwords or passwords that are easy to guess. Developing one-of-a-kind and complex passwords for each user account on your network is essential in safeguarding your network. Using a password manager can assist in the process of generating and securely storing passwords. Should You Hide Your SSID While Broadcasting It, or Should You Not? The name of your website is referred to as the Service Sat Identifier, or SSID for short. Some people believe that knowing the SSID improves network security because it makes the network less evident to others who might try to hack it. However, this strategy only provides low protection because dedicated hackers can still access unearthly skids. Maintaining the SSID broadcasting function while concentrating on other security measures is recommended. Access Control Lists, or acts, are used to restrict the devices that are authorized to access a network. Through access control lists, network administrators are granted the ability to decide which devices are permitted to connect to the network. Administrators can add a layer of protection to the system by preventing unauthorized devices from gaining access by maintaining a list of allowed MAC devices and preventing unauthorized devices from gaining access. Regular firmware updates, often known as patches, fix vulnerabilities. Firmware upgrades are regularly made available for download by manufacturers of routers and access points to resolve potential security flaws. Maintaining the most reliable version of your network equipment is necessary to patch any known vulnerabilities and protect against any developing threats. Separation for Enhanced Safety in Guest Networks The construction of guest networks is supported by many wireless routers. Visitors will access the institute through its separate networks but remain disconnected from the leading network. While simultaneously providing customers with ease, this product gives illegal access to essential data. Monitoring for suspicious activity is the function of intrusion detection systems (IDS). Intrusion detection systems can recognize and report potentially dangerous or suspicious actions to network administrators. Installing an intrusion detection system (IDS) assists in the early detection and rapid response to potential attacks.

SQL Injection: A Practical Overview

1. Introduction: sq. injection demystified

Sq. injection has a well-developed reputation for being one of web applications' most common security flaws. This attack vector becomes active when an application does not sufficiently sanitize user-generated input for sq. queries. What is the result? Criminals can very quickly inject malicious sq. code into a database, which can then interfere with database processes and cause enormous harm.

2. Mechanics of sq. injection

To fully comprehend sq. injection, a fundamental understanding of sq., also known as a structured query language, is required. For database manipulation, sq. is the universal language. In most cases, sq. queries are utilized by web applications to retrieve, insert, or use other database queries. An attacker will typically do an sq. injection by injecting malicious sq. code into a target website's form fields, urn parameters, or even HTTP headers. The database will carry out the malicious sq. code once the application has incorporated this input into sq. queries without performing any validation.

3. Forms of sq. injection

- ## Union-based injection:

This requires using the union SQL operator to combine the outcomes of the initial query with the effects of one or more subsequent subsequences.

- ## Error-based injection

The attacker causes SQL mismatches in this attack stage, exposing confidential database information.

- ## Time-based blind injection:

This relies on pausing the database for a predetermined amount of time to validate the attacker's hypothesis about the nature of vulnerability.

4. Mitigating sq. injection

- ## Prepared statements:

Utilizing parameterized queries is one of the most effective ways to reduce vulnerability to sq. injection attacks. sa

- **Stored procedures:**
Another viable strategy is protecting against sq. injection vulnerabilities by utilizing the database's stored procedures.

- **Input validation**
Utilize frameworks that do not permit the use of very relevant characters in sq. injection, such as single quotes, double quotes, and semicolons.

5. Moral issues

Even though ethical hackers use sq. injection to find vulnerabilities, they need to stay within the legal bounds that have been established. Before carrying out any penetration testing, you must first seek permission.

Finding Weaknesses

Finding vulnerabilities in a system and taking advantage of them is an essential part of ethical hacking in the ever-changing cybersecurity environment. It entails thoroughly identifying vulnerabilities within systems, networks, and applications before bad actors can exploit their flaws. This proactive approach to security is necessary for protecting digital assets' integrity and safeguarding sensitive information.

1. The Significance of Vulnerability Assessment

To get started with our initiative, it is necessary to understand why vulnerability awareness is the foundation of ethical hacking. The digital environment is riddled with possible vulnerabilities, each of which hackers might use to their advantage. Faulty software, incorruptible systems, or human mistakes may have caused these vulnerabilities. To practice security breaches, locating the areas of vulnerability and taking corrective action is necessary.

2. Methodologies for Finding Weaknesses

- Ethical hackers utilize various attack vectors and strategies to uncover vulnerabilities effectively. Automated scanning with specific tools is one method that can be used among many others. These programs can perform vulnerability scans on networks and systems to identify known flaws and provide detailed reports on their findings. On the other hand, they can only recognize recognized problems, so they might also look for previously unknown dangers. Testing using manual procedures is yet another essential practice. Hackers with ethical intentions carefully examine computer systems, software programs, and source code to find security flaws that automated methods could miss. It is crucial to have this personal touch to detect subtle or customized defects.

3. Common Vulnerabilities and Attack Vectors

Ethical hackers must have a solid understanding of typical attack routes and vulnerabilities. The following are examples of common types of vulnerabilities:

- **Weak Passwords:**

When it comes to cyber security, passwords are frequently the weakest link. Hackers with a moral code may employ password cracking and brute-force attacks to discover critical security flaws.

- **Unpatched Software**

Outdated software may still have previously discovered vulnerabilities. Ethical hackers actively look for computer systems that run software that has not been updated.

- **Injection Attacks**
Injection techniques, such as SQL injection and code injection, are used to modify inputs and gain unwanted access

4. The Importance of Responsible Disclosure

Responsibility disclosure is necessary if ethical hackers discover vulnerabilities. This involves notifying the organization or developer responsible for the system or program about the vulnerabilities that have been found. Because of this, they can patch the vulnerabilities before a lousy actor can take advantage of them. Responsible disclosure is an ethical obligation that must be followed in the area of ethical hacking.

5. The Role of Continuous Monitoring

The process of assigning vulnerabilities is not an on-time activity. The digital landscape is constantly shifting, resulting in the emergence of new vulnerabilities regularly. Therefore, regular monitoring is required to ensure that a solid security posture is always maintained. Ethical hackers and security experts are responsible for maintaining a state of vigilance and adjusting their techniques in response to changing dangers.

6. Legal and Ethical Considerations

Ethical hacking occurs within the confines of a set of rules, both moral and legal. Accessing computer systems or networks without proper authorization is both unlawful and unethical. Before conducting vulnerability assessments, ethical hackers are always required to secure the appropriate permission. In addition, they are responsible for ensuring that their actions do not compromise the system's security or interfere with its regular operation.

System Capture: Exploitation

1. System Capture: Exploitation in the Realm of Ethical Hacking

Exploiting computer systems is a crucial step in the complex ethical hacking process, one of the many complicated steps. This phase, frequently referred to as "system capture," is a crucial moment when an ethical hacker attempts to gain unauthorized access to a target system by imitating the methods criminals could use. Within this discussion, we will dive into the complexity of system exploration, emphasizing its significance, methodologies, and ethical implications.

2. The Significance of System Exploitation

Ethical hacking relies heavily on system exploitation, which serves a dual purpose and is a fundamental component of the fiddle. In the first place, it reveals flaws in a target system, enabling businesses and other organizations to fix these problems before malicious actors take advantage of them. Second, it provides ethical hackers with an in-depth grasp of cybercriminals' methods, improving their ability to defend themselves. The symbiotic link between hacking and security shows the significance of exploiting system vulnerabilities.

3. Methods of System Exploitation

Exploiting a system can involve various methods and approaches, each of which has its own modus operandi. In this section, we will focus on a handful of the most prominent ones:

- **Buffer Overflow Attacks:**

This time-honoured method takes advantage of the fact that programs are susceptible to information overload. Hackers can execute arbitrary code and take control of the system if they overflow a buffer assigned for that purpose.

- **Privilege Escalation:**

Within a system that has been penetrated, ethical hackers frequently attempt to increase their privileges.

66

Acquiring higher access rights, which pave the way for more in-depth study and manipulation, is required for this stage.

- **Zero-Day Exploits:**
Undisclosed vulnerabilities in software or hardware are referred to as zero-day vulnerabilities. An ethical hacker can gain a significant advantage by exploiting such vulnerabilities, as the developers are unaware of the consequences and, as a result, have not been corrected.

- **Malware Injection:**
Infiltrating a system with malicious code is a popular strategy used by cybercriminals. Trojan horses, viruses, and other malware can penetrate a plan and put its security at risk.

4. Ethical Considerations

Within ethical hacking, specialists are held to an extremely high standard of ethics that controls their behaviour. When engaging in activities that involve the exploration of computer systems, it is essential to adhere to the following ethical guidelines:

- **Authorized Access Only:**
Before engaging in any system exploration, ethical hackers must first get the explicit consent of the system's owners.

- **Data Protection:**
Even as the data is being exploited, the privacy and confidentiality of the sensitive information must be maintained at all times.

- **Minimal Disruption:**
Ethical hackers should cause as little disruption as possible to the target system to avoid causing any downtime for the business.

Privilege Escalation: Promotion

Privilege escalation is a fundamental technique in computer security that describes how an adviser or user acquires higher levels of access and control within a computer system or network than initially permitted. It is important because it refers to a process that cybercriminals can exploit. It is a powerful method that malicious actors frequently utilize and is commonly used to compromise the security and integrity of systems. In this discussion, we will go into the complexity of private escalation, its many different manifestations, and the strategies that can be utilized to combat this ever-present danger.

1. Understanding Privilege Levels

It is vital to have a solid understanding of privilege levels in computer systems before digging further into the concept of privilege escalation. Most contemporary operating systems use a hierarchy of privileges to ensure that users or processes can only carry out activities for which they have been granted permission. These labels are often broken down into the following categories:

- **Administrator Privileges:**

In computer systems that use the UNIX operating system, administrative privileges, often known as "root" privileges, are granted to system administrators. They can carry out actions that regular users cannot, such as configuring the system, installing software, and making modifications to existing system files.

2. Types of Privilege Escalation

The escalation of a vehicle can be broken down into two basic categories: vertical escalation and horizontal escalation. Both of these types of private escalation can occur.

- **Vertical Privilege Escalation**

During a virtual escalation, a user or an attacker moves their privileges from a lower level (such as a regular user) to a higher level (such as an administrator). Vertical escalation is a form of privileging escalation. This privilege escalation is among the most painful because it grants access to essential data and components of the system.

- **Horizontal Privilege Escalation**

In horizontal escalation, a hacker or user who already possesses a specific privilege level tries to get into another user's account with the same degree of privilege. Even though this escalation method is not as strict as vertical escalation, it still has the potential to result in unauthorized access and data breaches.

3. Common Methods of Privilege Escalation

It is possible to escalate privileges using various methods, each taking advantage of a unique vulnerability or misconfiguration within a system. The following are some examples of frequent ways:

- **Exploiting Software Vulnerabilities:**
Attackers may exploit software vulnerabilities such as buffer overflows or code injection to execute malicious code with enhanced privileges.

4. Mitigating Privilege Escalation

A multipronged strategy that adds prevention, detection, and reaction to privilege escalation risks is necessary to mitigate the privilege escalation risk effectively. The following are some methods that can strengthen the system's security:

- **Real-World Examples**
A common thread that runs through significant cyber security events is the elimination of privileges gained by an attacker. A good illustration of this is the "Stunt" worm, which specifically targeted Iran's nuclear program. As an example of the devastation that may result from successful privilege escalation assaults, the computer worm Stunt took advantage of many modern-day vulnerabilities to acquire control of industrial control systems and establish its access privileges. One such illustration of this would be the

"heartbleed" vulnerability in the Opens library, making it possible for attackers to steal sensitive data directly from memory. Although this was not a private escalation attack in the conventional sense, it brought to light how critical it is to resolve security flaws in order to prevent unauthorized access rapidly.

After Exploitation: Captured

- **Post-Exploitation: Maneuvering in Captured Territory**

After experimentation, ethical hackers call it "captured territory." Ethical hackers, or penetration testers, enter the target system to steal or safeguard data. This discussion will include non-copyrighted post-exploitation strategies and methods.

- **The Landscape of Captured Territory**

Consider a committed system with data, permissions, and control pieces. Like a chess player, the ethical hacker moves gracefully through this landscape. This project must use non-copyrighted methods to remain authentic.

- **Maintaining Stealth**

In captured territory, avoiding detection is critical. This requires continuous methods to monitor the compromised system without detection. Rootkits can hide the hacker's existence, allowing prolonged surveillance and data filtration.

- **Privilege Escalation**

When working within a system that has been compromised, removing privileges is frequently a necessary step. Acquiring higher-level permissions, which can grant access to sensitive data and essential functions, is crucial. Techniques for non-copyrighted privilege escalation include the detection of system vulnerabilities and the prudent exploration of those weaknesses. Examples of system vulnerabilities include incorrect transmissions or unpatched software.

- **The Arsenal of Tools**

When operating in captured territory, ethical hackers can access various tools not protected by intellectual property laws. Without leaving a trace behind, these instructions are meant to make surveillance, last-minute movement, and data retrieval easier.

- **Meterpreter**

Meterpreter is a widely used post-exploitation framework that is also an open-source application that provides a variety of capabilities. These features include network surveys, process control, and file system manipulation. It acts continuously, causing the slightest disturbance possible with the system being targeted.

- **PowerShell Empire**

Another powerful tool explicitly developed for post-exploitation activities is called powershell Empire. It does this by utilizing the lightweight Windows scripting language, powerShell, which allows it to carry out operations and collect information consistently. It is less probable that security measures will be tampered with by the use of powershell because it is a native component of Windows.

- **Ethical Considerations**

Ethical hackers must adhere to strict ethical guidelines throughout the post-exploitation phase. The non-copyrighted principles of ethical hacking emphasize the significance of giving authority, receiving informed consent, and ensuring that the tasting method does not cause any harm or damage to the target.

Social Engineering: Manipulation

- **Unveiling the Art of Social Engineering: Manipulating Minds and Actions**

The practice of social engineering is one of the most potent weapons that bad actors have at their disposal in the field of cyber security, which is characterized by a never-ending struggle for the protection of data and information. In this context, social engagement is considered one of the most effective weapons. Social engineering is a form of hacking that, in contrast to more traditional methods of computer intrusion, which focus on exploiting software flaws, targets the human element by taking advantage of people's predisposition to trust, cooperate, or give in to psychological manipulation. In this discussion, we will tour the complex trajectories of social engagement, illuminating the numerous strategies and psychological mechanisms that advisers utilize to exert influence over individuals and organizations.

- **Understanding the Foundations**

At its most fundamental level, social engineering is manipulating individuals to obtain personal information, provide unauthorized access, or carry out acts that are advantageous to the attacker. To have a proper appreciation for the efficacy of this method, it is necessary to understand the psychological foundations that make it possible. People are naturally social creatures who are hardwired to form relationships based on trust and approval while avoiding conflict at all costs. Social engineers use people's natural talents to behave in specific ways.

- **The Techniques of Manipulation**

Social engineers have a toolbox with methods, each of which has been painstakingly developed to practice a particular psychological weakness. Techniques such as practising, baiting, phishing, tailgating, and quid pro quo are examples of some of the most frequent practices. The act of fabricating a situation, also known as pretexting, to coerce a target into disclosing information entails the use of the pretexting technique. Impersonating a respected authority figure or a staff member at a recognized institution is a standard method used in this scheme. The term "baiting" refers to luring users into a trap by providing them with something appealing, such as free software or downloads, which are, in reality, a vehicle for distributing malware. Phishing is possibly the most common method by which attackers pose as legitimate entities, most frequently through email, to obtain sensitive data or confidential information. Phishing is used to steal login information. Tailgating involves using people's natural inclination to hold doors open for others. An intruder can gain unlawful access to a restricted area by following an employee into the room. Providing a benefit or service in exchange for information is known as "quid pro quo." An adviser could, for instance, pretend to be an IT assistant and offer to resolve a problem that does not exist in exchange for login credentials.

- **Psychological Manipulation: The Key to Success**

The skilful management of psychological techniques is essential to successful social engineering. Respect is one of the fundamental principles that is taken advantage of. The tendency to show gratitude and return a favour or consequence is hardwired into the human psyche. When an attacker provides something beneficial to the target, the target will frequently feel driven to give information or comply with a request to "return the favour."

Authority is a powerful psychological tool in its own right. People tend to obey those in authority without questioning their actions. Social engineers take advantage of this by posing as authoritative figures, such as managers, members of the information technology staff, or law enforcement officials.

Further, the risk of experiencing unfavourable outcomes effectively drives behaviour change. Social engineers employ various forms of coercion and intimidation to coerce their targets into complying with their wishes. They may resort to punitive actions or disclosing humiliating information to exert pressure on their victims.

- **The Human Element: Weakest Link or Last Defense?**

The human factor is still the weakest link in the chain of defences against cyber-attacks, despite modern technology and firewalls being used to strengthen these protections. No matter how solid the digital devices may be, a skilled social engineer can frequently locate a psychological vulnerability in the system and exploit it to break through. However, this weakness can also act as the final line of defence in an attack. Organizations can equip their workers to recognize and thwart such attacks if they educate their employees and individuals on social engineers' strategies and psychological techniques. This education can take the form of training sessions. The best defence against social engineering is vigilance, healthy scepticism, and a dedication to confirming results. These things can go a long way.

Dodos Attacks and Mitigation

The plague of distributed denial of service (Dodos) attacks has spread throughout the digital world, posing severe dangers to individual organizations and businesses. I will elaborate on Dodo's assaults and various mitigation measures academically to thoroughly discuss this issue while conforming to your standards. This will allow me to handle this topic while sticking to my requirements entirely.

- ## The Unrelenting Challenge: Dodos Attacks

Distributed denial of service attacks, also known as Dodos assaults, are malicious activities that are carried out in the digital age with the intention of crippling internal services and making them inaccessible to people who are authorized to use them. These assaults are distinguished by their scattered nature, which lends them a fragile quality and makes it challenging to repel them. A Distributed Denial of Service Attack It is common practice to refer to the network of infected devices that exposes Dodos attacks as a "botnet." These infected devices, which are now under the control of cybercriminals, are forced to generate an enormous volume of traffic aimed at the server or network that is the focus of the attack. The goal is to deplete the target's resources, which will result in a degradation of their service or in it becoming completely unavailable. Attacks Using Different Dodos Variants

- **Volumetric Attacks:** They flood the target with enormous traffic, which completely obstructs their bandwidth capabilities.
- **Protocol Attacks:** They can interrupt communication between the

target and its users by taking advantage of vulnerabilities in the network protocols.

- **Application Layer Attacks:** They want to deliver services by focusing on particular apps or services.

- **Mitigation Strategies**

A multipronged strategy that integrates proactive planning, network architecture and real-time monitoring is required to combat the threat posed by distributed denial of service assaults (Dodos). In the following, we will outline many successful ways to protect against Dodos attacks:

- **Traffic Scrubbing and Filtering:** Scrubbing and filtering solutions can help identify and eliminate harmful traffic from the incoming data stream, and their implementation is recommended for this purpose. Because of this strategy, the network is effectively cleared of unnecessary traffic, allowing legal traffic to reach its destination.

- **Content Delivery Networks (CDN):** Using content delivery networks (CDN) allows traffic to be distributed across numerous services, which reduces the impact of distributed denial of service assaults (Dodos). By routing traffic and caching content closer to users, content delivery networks (cans) can absorb and mitigate attacks.

- **Rate Limiting and Access Control Lists (ACLs):** It is possible to restrict the amount of traffic an attacker may generate by setting limits and deploying access control lists on routers and firewalls. This will effectively reduce the impact that distributed denial of service attacks have.

- **Anomaly-Based Intrusion Detection Systems (IDS)** Deploying IDS that can identify abnormal traffic patterns can help in the early detection of Dodos attacks, allowing for timely counts.

- **Cloud-Based Dodos Protection Services:**

Cloud-based distributed denial of service (Dodos) protection services, which various service providers offer, can absorb attack traffic in the cloud by protecting the target infrastructure from the assault. Cloud-based distributed denial of service (Dodos) protection services, which are offered by various service providers, can absorb attack traffic in the cloud by protecting the target infrastructure from the assault.

Career Prospects: Exploring Professional Avenues

- ## Exploring Professional Avenues in Ethical Hacking

The ever-changing nature of the digital economy has resulted in an increased demand for experts who can protect our intricately interconnected world. One of the most critical aspects of cyber security is ethical hacking, sometimes called penetration testing or whistle-hat hacking. The purpose of this chapter is to take you on a tour of the numerous professional opportunities available to individuals who enter the world of ethical hacking.

- ## Ethical Hacking: A Necessity in Modern Cybersecurity

Before getting into the vast diversity of job prospects, it is essential to have a solid understanding of why ethical hacking has become such an important part of modern cyber security. The attack space available to hostile actors has significantly expanded due to the expansion of online services, cloud computing, and the Internet of Things (IoT). As a direct result, more and more businesses are beginning to acknowledge the significance of practising security measures. Ethical hackers are an essential component in the process of strengthening digital devices. These hackers have a comprehensive awareness of vulnerabilities and exploits, giving them an advantage over other types of hackers. They find vulnerabilities in computer systems, apps, and networks, which enable businesses to fix the problems and prevent malicious hackers from taking advantage of the vulnerabilities they find. This practical method of adding cyber security concerns protecting sensitive data and ensuring that digital ecosystems maintain their unaltered state.

- **Career Paths in Ethical Hacking**

- **Penetration Tester:**

Carr's in ethical hacking is only getting started, and the people leading the charge are penetration testers, sometimes called ethical hackers. They are tasked with simulating cyber-attacks on an organization's systems to search for vulnerabilities and flaws that criminal actors might exploit. When conducting a comprehensive risk analysis of an organization's security posture, penetration testers use various testing tools and methods.

- **Security Analyst**

The organization gives security analysts the job of surveilling an organization's security infrastructure. Logs are analyzed, security issues are identified, and these individuals develop initiatives to improve security measures. Their contributions are essential in locating and neutralizing any security risks in real-time.

- **Security Consultant**

Companies that are looking to strengthen their cyber security posture often hire security consultants so that they can benefit from their experience. They analyze the current security frameworks, suggest enhancement, and offer assistance in implementing security solutions. To be successful in this capacity, you needed an in-depth knowledge of cyber security principles and the ability to communicate complex ideas to stakeholders who were not technically organized.

- **Incident Responder**

When there is a break in security, influential respondents are the first people on the scene to respond. They were entrusted with instigating security breaches, assessing the scope of the violations, and adopting measures to control and destroy environmental dangers. In this job, you need to respond quickly and strategically to limit potential damage.

- **Security Architect**

Information systems that are both reliable and secure are what security architects create. They design the blueprints for the security architecture and ensure that all components are robust enough to withstand any possible attacks. To be successful in this profession, you will need an in-depth knowledge of security protocols and technology.

- **Cyber security Trainer**

Individuals and companies can receive instruction from cybersecurity trainers to learn the industry's recommended procedures. They engage people in the field by developing training programs, conducting workshops, and disseminating information through these activities. To cultivate a culture of cyber security awareness, this function is necessary.

- **Educational and Certification Requirements.**

To get started in ethical hacking, you will need a strong educational foundation and certifications in the necessary areas. A bachelor's degree in computer science, computer security, or a closely related topic is an essential foundation for beginning your career. On the other hand, it is necessary to supplement academic knowledge with experience in the real world. Certifications that have earned a high level of respect within the sector include Certified Ethical Hacker (CEH), Certified Information Systems Security Professional (CISSP), and Offensive Security Security Professional (OSCP). Certifications like these certify one's skills and boost employability simultaneously. Sectors of the Industry: Ethical hackers can get work in a variety of industries, which opens up a lot of doors for them. The following are some of the most essential industries:

- **Remuneration**

The amount of money that ethical hackers make might vary widely based on several criteria, like their experience level, certifications, and location. The pay offered by enterprise-level roles is usually competitive, whereas the incomes experienced by ethical hackers and specialists may command might be substantial. In addition, freelance ethical hackers frequently charge on a project-by-project basis, allowing them to make consistent amounts for their expenses. This document is known as the Ethical Hacker's Code of Conduct. Even if there is a lot of opportunity for growth in ethical hacking, it is crucial to stress how vital accountability and ethics are in this line of work. Ethical hackers adhere to a tight code of conduct that emphasizes their abilities' legitimacy and responsive application. They are required to obtain the appropriate authorization before carrying out security assessments, and they are expected to protect the privacy and confidentiality of both individuals and businesses.

Windows Systems: Understanding the Flaws

- **Windows Systems: Unveiling Vulnerabilities and Exploits**

Windows operating systems, ubiquitous in the digital world, provide an ideal environment for increased productivity and, regrettably, more opportunities for exploration. To understand the vulnerabilities that Windows systems are known to have, we will go on a trip through a labyrinth of vulnerabilities. Our goal is to strengthen our defences while ethically hacking through the complications of this ubiquitous platform.

- **The Foundation: Windows Operating Systems**

Recognizing the variety of Windows operating systems, ranging from older editions such as Windows 95 to the most up-to-date version, Windows 11, is essential to developing awareness of the vulnerabilities that exist in Windows. Every iteration introduces a brand-new set of vulnerabilities, each of which has the potential to be exploited.

- **User Account Control (UAC): A Blessing and a Curse**

Users are prompted for administrator rights when there is a need to make changes to the system via UAC, which was meant to improve system security. However, savvy attackers may utilize UAC to achieve higher privileges, making it both a security benefit and a possible vulnerability. UAC's dual nature allows it to be seen as either a security flaw or a potential weakness. Service Vulnerabilities Are the Weakest Link in the Chain

- **Service Vulnerabilities: The Achilles' Heel**

Windows services, which are necessary for the system's operation, might serve as entry points for malicious actors. Malware, like Winery, is infamous for exploiting security holes in commonly used protocols and services, such as the Server Massage Block (SMB) protocol, which results in significant disruption.

- **Patch Management: The Race Against Time.**

Patches are often made available by Microsoft to remedy previously discovered flaws. Despite this, the race between the distribution of patches and their exploitation continues. Handling updates and patches promptly is essential since delayed updates might leave systems vulnerable to known attacks.

- **Legacy Software and Compatibility: A Double-Edged Sword**

Windows may introduce the vulnerabilities of older software while still maintaining compatibility with it. Old codebases that have not been updated to reflect new security best practices might be a fertile breeding ground for vulnerabilities.

- **User Habits and Social Engineering** Errors made by humans may threaten the safety of even the most well-protected system. The vulnerability of users to social engineering assaults like phishing may lead to breakdowns in technological neighbourhoods that are otherwise impenetrable.

- **Remote Desktop Protocol (RDP): A Gateway to Intrusion**

RDP, developed for accessing remote systems, is exploitable if its configuration is incorrectly done.

Attackers can acquire illegal access, which might result in data breaches or loss of system control.

- **Privilege Escalation: Ascending the Hierarchy**

Vulnerabilities that allow attackers to gain enhanced privileges in Windows are highly sought. Because of these vulnerabilities, they can increase their user rights and take control of the system, which often results in total penetration. Malware and Trojan Horses: Invisible Intruders There is a lot of malicious software created specifically for Windows computers. These malicious programs, which ranged from Trojans to rootkits, were designed to exploit Windows vulnerabilities for various negative reasons, including data theft and systems compromise.

- **Exploits and Zero-Day Vulnerabilities**

The first step in securing Windows is to familiarize oneself with its vulnerabilities. Utilizing best practices such as often performing updates, using a robust authentication method, and operating intrusion detection systems may drastically reduce the danger of exploitation. Antivirus Software and Protection for Endpoints Antivirus software and other endpoint security solutions play the role of safeguards, guarding against known threats and malware. Even though they are not infallible, they give another layer of protection to the system. Firewalls and intrusion detection systems (IDS) are two types of network security. Firewalls and intrusion detection systems (IDS) are crucial elements in the protection of networks. They are capable of providing unwanted access and identifying suspicious behaviours if they are received correctly. Education and Instruction of the Users The process of educating people about possible dangers and safe computing habits can completely transform the game. Attacks that use social engineering have a lower chance of succeeding if users are vigilant.

www.ingramcontent.com/pod-product-compliance
Lightning Source LLC
LaVergne TN
LVHW051535050326
832903LV00033B/4263